A BRIEF ANTHOLOGY OF

Byron Katie's Words

A BRIEF ANTHOLOGY OF

Byron Katie's Words

Edited by Stephen Mitchell

the work of
byron katie
WWW.THEWORK.ORG

BYRON KATIE INTERNATIONAL, INC. • *LOS ANGELES*

Published in the United States by
Byron Katie International, Inc.
P.O. Box 2110
Manhattan Beach, CA 90267
www.thework.org

ISBN 1-890246-02-6

Design by Jeffrey Ainis & Andrew Bernstein

For you

Introduction

In 1986, after many years of deep depression, Byron Katie had a spontaneous insight into the human mind. She saw that when she believed her thoughts, she suffered, and that when she didn't believe her thoughts, she didn't suffer. Instantly, her mind released its painful arguments with reality the way a hand would drop a hot object, and Katie found herself filled with a freedom and joy beyond description. Without a story about how things should be, she saw that everything is perfect and beautiful just the way it is.

For several years after her initial insight, Katie continued to experience ongoing revelations about the mind, the human condition, how we cause our own suffering, and the power of unconditional love. She realized that many of our most cherished beliefs about the world were completely backward. As people approached Katie to ask how they too could experience such happiness, she began to teach them to investigate their thoughts with a simple yet powerful method she called The Work. The Work is fully explained in Katie's book, *Loving What Is.*

People seeking a way out of their suffering have found great value in Katie's ability to address the most profound subjects in a direct, simple, and understandable way, free of any dogma. They have also appreciated Katie's open heart and sense of humor.

The sayings collected here by Stephen Mitchell are a small yet representative sample of Katie's words. Sit with them and see where they take you. Use them as springboards for your own realizations. As Katie says, "Until you realize something for yourself, it's not yours. And it's not fully yours until it lives through you as clear and loving action."

A BRIEF ANTHOLOGY OF

Byron Katie's Words

if you want reality to be different than it is, you might as well try to teach a cat to bark. You can try and try, and in the end the cat will look up at you and say, "Meow." Wanting reality to be different than it is is hopeless. You can spend the rest of your life trying to teach a cat to bark.

I am a lover of what is, not because I'm a spiritual person, but because it hurts when I argue with reality. No thinking in the world can change it. What is is. Everything I need is already here now. How do I know I don't need what I want? I don't have it. So everything I need is supplied.

through inquiry, we discover how attachment to a belief or story causes suffering. Before the story there is peace. Then a thought enters, we believe it, and the peace seems to disappear. We notice the feeling of stress in the moment, investigate the story behind it, and realize that it isn't true. The feeling lets us know that we are opposing what is by believing the thought. It tells us that we're at war with reality. When we notice that we're believing a lie and living as if it were true, we become present outside our story. Then the story falls away in the light of awareness, and only the awareness of what really is remains. Peace is who we are without a story. Until the next stressful story appears. Eventually inquiry becomes alive in us as the natural, wordless response of awareness to the thoughts and stories that arise.

my experience is that confusion is the only suffering. Confusion is when I argue with what is. When I am perfectly clear, what is is what I want. So when I want something that's different from what is, I'm very confused.

The Work always brings us back to who we really are. Each belief investigated to the point of understanding allows the next belief to surface. You undo that one. Then you undo the next, and the next. And then you find that you are actually looking forward to the next belief. At some point, you may notice that you're meeting every thought, feeling, person, and situation as a friend. Until eventually you are looking for a problem. Until, finally, you notice that you haven't had one in years.

a feeling is like the mate to a thought appearing. It's like a left and a right. If you have a thought, there's a simultaneous feeling. And an uncomfortable feeling is like a compassionate alarm clock that says, "You're caught in the dream. Wake yourself up!" But if we don't honor the alarm clock, then we try to alter and manipulate the feeling by reaching into an apparent external world. We're usually aware of the feeling before the thought. That's why I say the feeling is an alarm clock that lets you know you're in a thought that you may want to investigate. If it's not acceptable to you, if it's painful, you might want to inquire and do The Work.

You are love.
It hurts to
believe you're
other than who
you are, to live
any story
less than
love.

when you are mentally out of your business, you experience immediate separation, loneliness, and fear. If you're lonely or sad, you may want to ask yourself, "Whose business am I in mentally?" And you may come to see that you've never been present, that you've mentally been living in other people's business all your life. Just to notice that you're in someone else's business can bring you back to your wonderful self. What a sweet place to be. Home.

there are no physical problems — only mental ones.

depression, pain, and fear are gifts that say, "Sweetheart, take a look at your thinking in this moment. You're living in a story that isn't true for you." Living a lie is always stressful. And investigating a lie through The Work always leads you back to who you are. Who you are is not an option. You are love. It hurts to believe you're other than who you are, to live any story less than love.

attachment to a thought means believing the thought to be true. When we don't inquire, we assume that a thought is true, though we can't ever know that. The purpose of attachment is to keep us from the realization that we are already truth. We don't attach to things; we attach to our stories about things.

thoughts are friends, not enemies. They're just what is. They appear. They're innocent. We're not doing them. They're not personal. They're like the breeze or the leaves on the trees or the raindrops falling. They appear like that, and we can make friends with them. Would you argue with a raindrop? Raindrops aren't personal, and neither are thoughts. Once a painful concept is met with understanding, the next time it appears you may find it interesting. What used to be the nightmare is now just interesting. The next time it appears, you may find it funny. The next time, you may not even notice it. This is the power of loving what is.

There is no story
that is you or
that leads to you.
Every story
leads away
from you.
You are what
exists before all
stories.

if you understand the three kinds of business enough to stay in your own business, it could free your life in a way that you can't even imagine. The next time you're feeling stress or discomfort, ask yourself whose business you're in mentally, and you may burst out laughing! That question can bring you back to yourself. And you may come to see that you've never really been present, that you've been mentally living in other people's business all your life. And if you practice it for a while, you may come to see that *you* don't have any business either and that your life runs perfectly well on its own.

how do you react when you believe that
you shouldn't think certain thoughts, and you do?
Turn it around — you *should* think them! Does
that feel a bit lighter, a bit more honest? Out of the
straitjacket. Your nature is freedom. And in the peace
of that, the thoughts come through and they're not
meeting an enemy who is opposing them, like a child
who comes to her father and the father screams at
her, "Don't say that! Don't do that! You're wrong,
you're bad!" and punishes her every time she
approaches. What kind of father is that? Well, that's
the internal violence that keeps you from understanding. Would you meet a friend that way? Thoughts
are not enemies.

people often ask me if I'm an enlightened being. I don't know anything about that. I am just someone who knows the difference between what hurts and what doesn't. I am someone who only wants what is. To meet as a friend each concept that arose turned out to be my freedom. That's where The Work begins and ends — in me. The Work says, "Love it all, exactly as it is." And it shows you how. Wisdom is simply knowing the difference between what hurts and what doesn't hurt. There's immense freedom in that. It doesn't mean you have to do the right thing. It just allows you to quit fooling yourself and do what you do with some awareness. One way leads to suffering; the other way leads to peace.

concepts always separate us from reality. Concept: suffering. When you investigate, attachment to concepts can disappear, and peace is the result. Concepts are ageless. They're all that exists, and if you investigate, you don't even have *them*. Who told you "It's a sky"? You accepted it. You didn't go in and ask yourself. You didn't ask the one who knows. So now we're going inside and inquiring within ourselves and not waiting for the answers from outside.

I am the perpetrator of my suffering — but only all of it.

the world is your perception of it. Inside and outside always match — they are reflections of each other. The world is the mirror image of your mind. If you experience chaos and confusion inside, your external world has to reflect that. You have to see what you believe, because you are the confused thinker looking out and seeing yourself. You are the interpreter of everything, and if you're chaotic, what you hear and see has to be chaos. Even if Jesus, even if the Buddha were standing in front of you, you would hear confused words, because confusion would be the listener. You would hear only what you thought he was saying, and you'd start arguing with him the first time your story was threatened.

God's will and my will are the same, whether I notice it or not.

An uncomfortable
feeling is like
a compassionate
alarm clock
that says,
"You're caught in
the dream.
Wake yourself up!"

to think that we know what's best for another person is to be out of our business. The result is worry, anxiety, and fear. When we mentally step out of our business, we think that we know more than he, she, or God. The only real question is "Can we know what's right for ourselves?" That is our only business. And, as we eventually come to see, not even that.

"*mothers* are supposed to accept their daughters" — on what planet?! These concepts are like toys we've been playing with for eons, bouncing them around as if they were true, and we all know they're not.

you can't make a wrong decision; you can only experience the story arising about how you did it. I like to ask, "Are you breathing yourself?" No? Well, maybe you're not thinking yourself or making decisions either. Maybe it doesn't move until it moves, like a breath, like the wind. And you tell the story of how you are doing it to keep yourself from the awareness that you are nature, flowing perfectly. Who would you be without the story that you need to make a decision? If it's your integrity to make a decision, make it. And guess what? In five minutes, you might change your mind and call it "you" again.

in no way do I ever suggest that you drop a concept, that you drop your story. We have been taught forever that we need to control our thinking. I say, can we just meet it with a little understanding? We may as well: have you noticed? — here it comes again! Now. Now. Understanding is what we are left with on the other side of inquiry.

it's not your job to like me — it's mine.

an uncomfortable feeling is not an enemy. People say, "You have to be vigilant!" Well, that isn't my experience. I didn't have anyone to give me that teaching. What I had was a built-in vigilance — it's called a feeling. There's nothing I can do for it not to be there. It's grace. A painful feeling is a gift that says, "Get honest; inquire." We reach out for alcohol or television or credit cards, so we can focus out there and not have to look at the feeling. And that's as it should be, because in our innocence we haven't known how. So now what we can do is reach out for a paper and a pencil, write our thoughts down, and investigate them. A feeling is grace now that I know what to do with it. The feeling would come. I'd write down the nightmare I was in, in the moment. The feeling would change, and I didn't inquire in order to change the feeling. I did it for the love of truth. I fell in love. Good that it hurts — pain is the signal to do The Work.

decisions are easy. It's the story you tell about them that isn't easy. When you jump out of a plane and pull the parachute cord and it doesn't open, you feel fear, because you have the next cord to pull. So you pull that one, and it doesn't open. And that's the last cord. Now there's no decision to make. When there's no decision, there's no fear, so just enjoy the trip! And that's my position — I'm a lover of what is. What is: no cord to pull. It's already happening. Free fall. I have nothing to do with it.

eventually we're lit, walking down the street like this mad, happy woman! And a concept comes like "My mother doesn't love me," and we're just laughter! Because we're awake to that concept, and the next, and the next.

you can be in pain and be in heaven, or you can be in pain and suffer. How do you know you're supposed to be in pain? Because that's what's happening. When you can live without a story and embrace what is, even in pain, you're in heaven. When you're in pain and you tell the story that you shouldn't be in pain, you're in hell.

my own experience is that I live in completeness, and that all of us do. It is the peace I walk in. I don't know anything. I don't have to figure anything out. I gave up forty-three years of thinking that went nowhere, and now I can be in the Don't-know. This leaves nothing but peace and joy in my life. It's the absolute fulfillment of watching everything unfold in front of me as me.

after the moment of clarity I had many years ago, these thoughts would appear as though I were being hit by them. They would hit me in the middle of a store, in the middle of the mall. I'd attach to a story, and it was as if a meteor had hit the planet and demolished it. And the inquiry was alive. Who would I be without the story "I'm not supposed to be afraid"? And I was like a little child. I would ask perfect strangers to hold me. "I'm afraid now." "I'm afraid." "I'm really frightened." Everything — every man, woman, child, and breath of air — is about my freedom. It's reality giving me what I need to get honest one time. You might as well give yourself permission to be afraid — how long have you been withholding it? Twenty years? Thirty? Do you think it can get any worse *with* permission? There's nothing to lose. Nothing to lose but hell.

I'm a lover
of reality,
because I know
the freedom
and power
of being
that lover.

what is God's intention? Whose business is God's intention? To go mentally into God's business is to be immediately lonely. That is why I keep that solid center — God is good, God is everything. I always know his intention: It's exactly what is in every moment. In fact, "God" is another name for what is. I don't have to question it anymore. I'm no longer meddling in God's business. It's simple. God is good, God is everything. And from that basis it's clear that everything is perfect. Then, if we investigate, we lose even that. And that is intimacy. That is God itself. One with. One as. Itself.

any story that you tell about yourself causes suffering. There is no authentic story.

the four questions unraveled each story,
and the turnaround led back to the storyteller — me.
I am the storyteller. I become the story I tell myself.
And I am what lives prior to every story. Every story,
every thing is God: reality. It apparently emerges
from out of Itself, and appears as a life. It lives forever within the story, until the story ends. From out
of Itself I appeared as my story, until the questions
brought me home. I love it that inquiry is so unfail-
ing. Story; pain; investigation; no story. Freedom is
possible in every moment. This is The Work, the
Great Undoing.

don't pretend yourself beyond your evolution.

what does compassion look like?
At a funeral, you eat the cake — just eat the cake!
You don't have to know what to do. It's revealed to
you. Someone will come into your arms. It speaks.
You're not doing it. Compassion is not a doing.
Don't bother thinking about it; just eat the cake. If
you're connected through pain, you're just standing
or you're sitting. And if there's no pain, you're still
just standing or sitting. But one way you're comfortable, the other way you're not.

what is sacred for you? The concept you're
holding onto in the moment. It doesn't get any more
sacred than that. Isn't that what you worship? That's
what you're devoted to. Now. Now. Now. Inquire, and
know what's real.

only in this moment (which doesn't exist) are we in reality. Everyone can learn to live in the moment, *as* the moment, to love what is in front of you, to love it as you. The miracle of love comes to you in the presence of the uninterpreted moment. If you are mentally somewhere else, you miss real life.

I'm a lover of reality, because I know the freedom and power of being that lover. All I want is what is. That's it. My plan to change things could only leave me with less. Even a simple thought like "I'm not okay" can be depressing, because it's a flat-out lie. Even on my deathbed, I'm okay. That is the truth.

we buy a home for our children, for our bodies; we get a garage for our car; we have dog houses for our dogs; but we won't give the mind a home. And we treat it like an outcast. We shame it and blame it and shame it again. But if you let the mind ask its questions, then the heart will rise with the answer. And "rising" is just a metaphor. The heart will reveal the answer, and the mind can finally rest at home in the heart and come to see that it and the heart are one. That's what these four questions are about. You write down the problem and investigate, and the heart gives you the answer you've always known. Now notice the turnaround to yourself. This is humility. There's nothing else to do. Standing in a room, or sitting in a chair, just watch the story. If it's frightening or depressing, ask four questions, turn it around. Come home.

The miracle
of love
comes to you
in the presence
of the
uninterpreted
moment.

just let it be. You may as well; it is. Everything moves in and out at its own time. You have no control. You never have; you never will. You only tell the story of what you think is happening. Do you think you cause movement? You don't. It just apparently is, but you tell the story of how you had something to do with it. "I moved my legs. I decided to walk." I don't think so — inquire and see that it's just a story about what is. You know that you are going to move because everything is happening simultaneously. You tell the story before the movement, because you already are that. *It* moves, and you think that you did it. Then you tell the story of how you're going somewhere or how you're doing something. The only place you can play with is the story. That's the only game in town. It's a beginning.

people are not supposed to feel pain? On what planet?! That's not reality. The reality of it is that we do. Is there anyone here who hasn't felt pain? But in the face of it we'll stand there and say we shouldn't be feeling it. That's insane. How do you live when you believe the thought "My son shouldn't be feeling pain"? You say you twist yourself inside out. So you're a person in pain trying to teach someone how not to feel pain! There's no teacher there of anything but pain. How can I end my son's pain if I can't end my own? Hopeless. Who would you be without the story "My son shouldn't be feeling pain"? You might be someone without pain, selfless, a listener, and then there would be a teacher in the house. A Buddha in the house — the one that lives it.

you want to hurt in your mind the person who hurt you. You hurt him the way you perceive he hurt you. Hurt feelings, hurt body, discomfort of any kind can't have to do with someone else. That's the truth. Who is feeling the pain? Anyone who sincerely inquires can discover that — anyone who inquires for the love of truth. Until you see the world as totally innocent, you haven't truly seen your own innocence.

you say that your feeling bad will help your friend — I want to get this straight. Your feeling bad will give her a better life? Your pain will in some way serve her? How do you react when you believe the thought that you can feel someone else's pain, and that that's compassion? If I hurt for you, does it mean that I love you? I don't think so!

Until you see
the world as
totally innocent,
you haven't truly
seen your own
innocence.

without a teacher there was no one to tell me that thought was an enemy. So it was only natural that eventually I would meet each thought arising and welcome it as a friend. I can't meet you as an enemy and not feel it. So how could I meet a thought within me as an enemy and not feel it? When I learned to meet my thinking as a friend, I noticed that I met every human as a friend. Because what could you say that has not appeared within me as a thought? It's so simple.

there's no suffering in the world; there's only an uninvestigated story that leads you to believe it. There's no suffering in the world that's real. Isn't that amazing! Investigate and come to know it for yourself.

"you're supposed to love yourself" — is that true? How do you treat yourself when you believe the thought that you're supposed to love yourself, and you don't? Can you see a reason to drop the story? And I'm not asking you to drop your sacred concept. Who would you be without the story "I'm supposed to love myself"? No human knows what that looks like. "You're supposed to love others"? Just another toy — another toy of torture. What's the direct opposite? "You're not supposed to love others." Doesn't that feel a little more natural? You're not supposed to love others — not until you do. These sacred concepts, these spiritual ideas, always turn into dogma.

we only fear what we are — what we haven't
gone inside and taken a look at and met with understanding. If I think you might see me as boring, it
would frighten me, because I haven't investigated
that thought. So it's not people that frighten me, it's
me that frightens me. That's my job, to frighten me,
until I investigate and stop this fear for myself. The
worst that can happen is that I think you think about
me what I think about myself. So I am sitting in a
pool of me.

you don't experience anxiety unless you've
attached to a thought that isn't true for you. It's that
simple. You don't ever feel anxiety until you believe
that a thought is true, and it's not.

until there's peace within you, there is
no peace in the world, because you are the world,
you are the earth. The story of earth is all there is of
earth and beyond. When you're in dreamless sleep at
night, is there a world? Not until you open your eyes
and say "I." "I woke up." "I have to go to work." "I'm
going to brush my teeth." Until the "I" is born, no
world. When the "I" arises, welcome to the movie
of who you think you are. Get the popcorn, here it
comes! If you investigate it, and the "I" arises, there's
no attachment. It's just a great movie. And if you
haven't investigated, the "I" arises, it's body-identified,
you think it's real, you think there's an "I." Pure fan-
tasy. And if you attach to it, if you think you're that,
you may want to inquire.

we do only three things in life: we stand, we sit, we lie horizontal. Once we've found success, we'll still be sitting somewhere until we stand, and we'll stand until we lie down or sit again. Success is a concept, an illusion. Do you want the $3900 chair instead of the $39 one? Well, sitting is sitting. Without a story, we're successful wherever we are.

I know that everyone in the world loves me. I just don't expect them to realize it yet.

you can't have it, because you already *are* it. You already have what you want. You already are what you want. This is as good as it gets. It appears as this now. Perfect. Flawless. And to argue with that is to experience the lie. The Work can give you this wonderful awareness: the awareness of the lie and the power of truth. The beauty of what really is.

when you become a lover of what is, the war is over. No more decisions to make. I like to say, "I'm a woman with no future." No decisions to make, no future. All my decisions are made for me, as they're all made for you. You're just mentally telling the story of how you have something to do with it.

there is a sweetness about the earth. I call it reality. Someone once referred to me as the master of descension. He said, "I've heard of masters of ascension, but you are the master of descension." So, because I had no teacher, reality sounds like this: Fall in love with what is. Woman sitting in chair with cup of tea. That's as sweet as I want it, because that is what is. When you love what is, it becomes so simple to live in the world. The world is exactly as it should be. Everything is God. Everything is good.

There's no
suffering
in the world;
there's only an
uninvestigated
story that
leads you
to believe it.

people talk about self-realization, and this is it! Can you just breathe in and out? To hell with enlightenment! Who cares about enlightenment when you're happy right now? Just enlighten yourself to this moment. Can you just do that? And then, eventually, it all collapses. The mind merges with the heart and comes to see that it's not separate. It finds a home, and it rests in itself, as itself. It can't be threatened or scolded or frightened away. Until the story is met with understanding, there is no peace.

the ego is terrified of the truth. And the truth is that the ego doesn't exist.

The Work always leaves you with less of a story. Who would you be without your story? You never know until you inquire. There is no story that is you or that leads to you. Every story leads away from you. Turn it around; undo it. You are what exists before all stories. You are what remains when the story is understood.

life is a very nice place to be. I woke up here. I'm a lover of this. You're always going to get what you need, not what you think you need. Then you come to see that what you need *is* what you want. Then you come to want only what is. That way you always win, no matter what.

someone says, "Oh, it's a terrible day; I'm so depressed." He is the champion of suffering, saying that there's something wrong here, something less than beauty. It's the mirror image without a clue that it's just a mirror image. Just be the *is*, the storyless movement, the reflection — nothing more. And in that, the source is known and merged. The reflection moves without argument as God. And that is awareness, the joy of what people call the world and what I refer to as the image of God Itself dancing. Even the story of a problem, when it is investigated, is laughable. Even that is God.

whatever is going on is fine. It's fine until you think, "Oh, I have to do this for two more days, or five more years." Terror! Two more days? Five more years? No: just now. And now. And now. This is not about a destination. It's about being comfortable wherever you are now, under any circumstances, rather than trying to manipulate circumstances around you like age, disease, and death. No one has ever made it. No one has survived, ever. Survival is not the point. Until you're comfortable under any circumstances, your Work isn't finished. How do you know when your Work is done? When they attack you and you notice that you love them with all your heart, your Work is done.

I'll say things like, "Until I'm free to be happy in the presence of my worst enemy, my Work's not done." And people can hear that as a motive for doing The Work. It's not — it's an observation. If you do The Work with some kind of motive — of getting your wife back or getting sober — forget it! Do The Work for the love of truth, for the love of freedom. Isn't that what you want your wife for anyway? So that you can be happy and free? Well, skip that, and be happy and free now! You're it. You're the one. There's nothing else to do.

do you want to meet the love of your life? Look in the mirror.

people ask how I can live if nothing has any meaning and I'm no one. It's very simple. We are being lived. We're not doing it. Are you breathing yourself? That's the end of the story. Did *you* just put your hand on your face? Did you plan it? Without a story, we move quite well. Effortlessly. In perfect health. Fluidly, freely, with a lot of love. And without war, without resistance. This possibility can be very frightening for people who think that they have control. So investigate, and see how life goes on, so much more joyfully. Even in its apparent collapsing, I see only joy.

we are really alive when we live in non-belief — open, waiting, trusting, and loving to do what appears in front of us now.

if you knew how important you were — and without the story you come to know it — you would fragment into a billion pieces, and just be light. That's what these misunderstood concepts are for, to keep you from the awareness of that. The appearance of love, that's who you'd have to be if you knew it — just a fool, blind with love. It takes so much pain to live out of the light. I don't know how people do it for so long. It was so painful that I could only do it for forty-three years. Forty-three centuries.

your ego has to terrify you all the time, so that you can investigate and come home to yourself in the body. This is what we are all here to live. When we aren't attached to our thinking, when all the why's, when's, and where's let go of us, then what really is becomes visible.

The litmus test for
self-realization
is the
constant state
of gratitude.

the fear of death is the last smokescreen for the fear of love. When the mind thinks of death, it looks at nothing and calls it something, to keep from experiencing what it — the mind — really is. Every fear is the fear of love, because to discover the truth of anything is to discover that there is nobody, no doer, no me to create suffering or to identify with anything. And so, without any of that, there is just love.

people sometimes ask me why being called a teacher feels uncomfortable. "Teacher" implies that we all don't teach equally or have equal wisdom. And that's not true. Everyone has equal wisdom. It is absolutely equally distributed. No one is wiser than anyone else. There's no one who can teach you except yourself.

live in the Now? Even the thought
"Now" is a concept. Even as the thought completes
itself, it's gone, with no proof that it ever existed
other than as a concept that would lead you to
believe it existed, and now that one is gone too.
Even thought doesn't exist. That's why everyone
already has the quiet mind that they're seeking.

all pleasure is pain, until I understand. Then I am the pleasure I was seeking. I am
what I always wanted. Pleasure is a mirror image of
what we already have before we look away from what
really is. When we stop seeking pleasure, the beauty
concealed by the seeking becomes evident. It's so
simple and clear. What we wanted to find from
pleasure is simply what is left beyond all stories.

the illusion is the mirror image attaching to a concept or belief. The illusion is the ego thinking that it's separate. It's not. It goes where God — reality — goes. God is all of it. The ego has no options. It can protest all it wants, but if God moves, *it* moves.

self meeting itself — that's the deal. If I wait for God to enlighten me, it's not so easy. It can be a long wait — years, decades maybe. When I'm on my knees praying to God in all sincerity, *I'm* the one listening. Can I do what I've begged God to do? Can I hear myself? Who else is listening? I'm a lover of reality. Can I just listen to myself? And when I hear myself, there's no separation. If I want God to do it, I turn it around. And in the peace of that, I come to know the truth.

to me, reality is God, because it rules. How do I know that my brother should have died? He did. That's reality. That's what is. It doesn't wait for my vote or my opinion. And even that doesn't exist, because what is is the story of a past. What I love most about a story of the past is that it's over. That's why I'm a lover of reality. It's always kinder than the story.

the privilege of having no teacher is that there's no tradition, so there's nothing to attach to. It doesn't have to look like anything but what it is. It's just such a fool — it doesn't know anything but love. It's God delighted. It comes to take the mystery and the importance out of everything. It takes the push and the time out of it.

the voice within is what I honor. It's what I'm married to. This life doesn't belong to me. The voice says, "Brush your teeth." Okay. I don't know what for, I just move on through. It says, "Walk." Okay. I just keep moving. Someone says, "Will you come?" Okay. I'm just following orders. The beautiful thing about this is that it's fun. Because if I don't follow the order, it's okay too. This is a game about where it will take me if I do follow. For forty-three years I was at war out in the story. And then one day, in a moment of clarity, I found my way back home. And that's what we're doing here — inquiry. It comes out from source and it returns to source. It's such a gift. I was always merging into my stories, into my insanity. And then, one day, when I heard "Brush your teeth," it started coming back, and there was a receiver. And it opened, like a womb. It opened into that allowing, into the mystery. Each moment — new! "Brush your teeth." It doesn't sound very spiritual to me, but that's all it said. "Walk." It just opens and it becomes more of a listener. All marriage is nothing more than a metaphor of that marriage. And if I don't follow, if I tell it, "Later," I don't feel very comfortable. And then I come back and I brush my teeth. It becomes a thing that's timeless, because when you're opening to that, there's no time and space in it. It's just a "Yes. Yes. Yes." That's why I say, "Boundaries are an act of selfishness." I don't have any. When it says, "Jump," I jump. Because where I jump, I have nothing to lose. There's nothing more fun than following such an insane thing and saying "Yes" to it. You don't have anything to lose. You're dead already. You can afford to be a fool.

there is no beginning of time, only beginning of thought.

every word is the sound of God. Every word
is the word of God. There is nothing personal here.
And everything is personal. If the moon rises, it's for
you. You're the one watching it! (And that's just a
beginning.)

the litmus test for self-realization is the
constant state of gratitude. That's the energy. This
gratitude is not something a person can look for or
find. It comes from another direction. It takes us over
completely. It's so vast that it can't be dimmed or
overlaid with anything that could hide it. It's like its
own self. The short version would be God intoxicated
with God, Itself. The total acceptance and consump-
tion of itself reflected back in the same moment in
that central place that is like fusion — it's the beginning. What looks like the end is the beginning. And
when you think it can't get any better, it gets better. It
has to. That's a law.

Forgiveness is
discovering that
what you thought
happened,
didn't —
that there was
never anything
to forgive.

it's personal and it's not personal. It's personal in that the whole world is me — a mirror image that I am and love. Without it I'm bodiless. And it's not that I need to look, it's just that looking is such a delight. On the other hand, it's not personal, because I see nothing more than a mirror image. Until God — reality — moves, I have no movement. Every movement, every sound, every breath, every molecule, every atom is nothing more than a mirror image of God. So I don't move, I'm being moved. I don't do, I'm being done. I don't think, I'm being thought. I don't breathe, I'm being breathed. There is no me, there is nothing personal or real about it. Whenever you speak, it's God speaking. When a flower blooms, it's God. When an army marches, it's God. I see only God. Add one more "o" and you've got good. To me they're synonymous. How could I not love all that I am, all that you are? One me.

love is so vast within itself. It's where you die. You don't die into fear; you die into love. It's so vast that it will burn you up. It's so jealous and greedy for itself mirrored back that it will leave you nothing. And when you're feeling that if you don't give it away you'll die in it, it's so vast that there's nothing you can do with it. All you can do is be it.

if you find the internal work exciting, you'll come to look forward to the worst that can happen, because you won't find a problem that can't be healed from the inside. And it becomes a mystery that you ever thought there was a problem — ever. This is paradise found.

forgiveness means discovering that what you thought happened, didn't. Until you can see that there is nothing to forgive, you haven't really forgiven. No one has ever hurt anyone. No one has ever done anything terrible. There's nothing terrible except your uninvestigated thoughts about what happened. So whenever you suffer, inquire, look at the thoughts you're thinking, and set yourself free. Be a child. Start from the mind that knows nothing. Take your ignorance all the way to your freedom.

I experience the "I" arising, and I quake with the privilege of that, because the "I" is Its very self, being born. When the "I" arises, It is presenting Itself to Itself. Your name is the name of God. It's equal to "table." "I." "God."

until we know that death is equal to life, and that it comes in its own sweet way, perfectly, we're going to take on the role of God without the awareness of it, and it's always going to hurt. Whenever you interfere with a process mentally — in the name of life, humanity, anything; in other words, whenever you mentally oppose what is — you're going to experience sadness and apparent separation. There's no sadness without the story. What is is. You *are* it. You're not saving anyone; you're not killing anyone. The world doesn't depend on you.

we're not doing anything. Ultimately, we are being done. If I say, "I'm going to the store," I'm very clear that I am God going to God. "Store" is a word for God. "I" is a word for God. And "God" is a word for what is. When I say I love you, there's no personality talking. It's self-love: I'm only talking to myself. The way I experience it is that It is only talking to Itself. If I say, "Let me pour you some tea," It is pouring Its own tea for Itself, and the tea is Itself. It's so self-absorbed that It leaves no room for any other. Nothing. Not a molecule separate from Itself. That's true love. It's the ultimate self. There's no other existence. It's self-consuming always and loving it. It's a guiltless state. There's no one separate. In the apparent world of duality, people are going to see it as a you and a me, but in reality there is only one. And even that's not true.

something is better than nothing — is that true? Something — a word for God. Nothing — a word for God. The same. There's no preference. Haven't you noticed? Something. Nothing. "God" is a word. We could have used any word. They're all words for God. You attach meaning to a word, and welcome to genesis.

everything is equal. There is no this soul or that soul. There's only one. And that's the last story. There's only one. And not even that. It doesn't matter how you attempt to be disconnected, it's not a possibility. Any thought you believe is an attempt to break the connection. But it's only an attempt. It can't be done. That's why it feels so uncomfortable.

even so-called truths eventually fall away. Every truth is a distortion of what is. The last truth — I call it the last judgment — is "God is every-thing, God is good." Ultimately, of course, even this isn't true. But if it works for you, I say keep it and have a wonderful life.

Until the story
is met with
understanding,
there is
no peace.

awareness always focuses on something. It surfs it. It will notice a finger or a foot. It's like a swaying. Somewhere within it there's always a focus. The breath is like a surfing at the back of the tongue. It doesn't matter where the awareness is. The breath, the fingers, the toes. Like a heartbeat. Something going on all the time within it. There's nothing moving it, and it is perpetual motion. Its focus is itself. It is always present, like your heartbeat. It doesn't go faster or slower. It's the steady condition. It's nothing, and we want to call it something. Now it's a hand on my head. My elbow on the couch. My hands on my foot. My heart beating. My toes swaying to its natural rhythm. I notice that my fingers are doing the same, ever so slightly. It would be undetectable if I were attached to anything. And as I speak, the swaying continues. There's no sound, even though it appears that I'm talking. When I hear sound, it is silence also. The tongue hitting the top of the mouth. Lips coming together as it speaks. The chair holding me. Always held. Even in the walking, the earth holds her.

BYRON KATIE is the author of *Loving What Is: Four Questions That Can Change Your Life*, written with Stephen Mitchell. She teaches people around the world a revolutionary process of inquiry known as The Work. Several times a year, Katie offers The School for The Work, a nine-day course that has been called "the most powerful self-realization program on earth." She also offers Weekend Intensives in cities around the world. Her web site is www.thework.org.

STEPHEN MITCHELL, Katie's husband, is the author of more than thirty-five books of fiction, non-fiction, poetry, translations, and children's books. His bestselling *Tao Te Ching* has been called "definitive for our time," and his *Selected Rilke* has been called "the most beautiful group of poetic translations [the twentieth] century has produced." His web site is www.stephenmitchellbooks.com.